Finding God in the craziness of Life

Kathy Mulhern

Living the Good News, Inc.
Denver, CO

Book

3

Living the Good News, Inc.
A Division of The Morehouse Group
Editorial Offices
600 Grant Street, Suite 400
Denver, CO 80203

Editorial Staff: Joanne Youngquist, Kathleen Mulhern, Dirk deVries, Liz Riggleman,
   Sue MacStravic, Dina Gluckstern, Kathy Coffey
Prepress/Production Staff: Sue MacStravic, Noel Taylor, Val Price, Meg Sandoval Phillips
Cover Design and Layout: Val Price, Sue MacStravic
Illustrations: Carolyn Klass

Printed in the United States of America.

The scripture quotations used herein are from the Today's English Version ©American Bible Society 1996, 1971, 1976, 1992. Used by permission.

ISBN 0-8192-8007-0

Contents

introduction

Perplexed by the puzzles in your life? Wondering where God is? Come along; you're in good company.

Maybe you're in a church; maybe not. Maybe you've been raised to believe in God; maybe you haven't. If you're not looking for God, none of those other things matter much because God, who has all the time in the world, waits for your desire, your search, your welcome. It's not God's way to be in your face. Only when you turn around, looking for God, do you find that God has been pursuing you all the time.

If you *are* looking for God, well, then...*Finding God in the Craziness of Life* is for you. While this book doesn't wrap up God in a tidy package and hand it to you, it will tell of glimpses and sightings and God-tracks left for you to find. These meditations take an honest look at the craziness of life—at the dilemmas and challenges and quirky joys we run into every time we turn around. And there, in that craziness, God is waiting, wanting to be found.

Here's how to use this book in your search:

Each meditation begins with a scripture reference. Get a Bible and read the whole passage first, then return to the quoted verse to open your thoughts. Read the reflection, which is written to let the truth of scripture and crazy reality come face-to-face, allowing the truth to illumine reality.

Each reflection closes with a prayer starter, two or three sentences that help you begin to move your thoughts down, down,

down into the heart where they can become prayer. Build on those prayer starters until your conversations with God take you where you have never gone before.

These meditations do not give answers, drill you with doctrine, push or pull. They simply entertain the possibility, the glorious chance, that God is near, very near indeed, hoping you'll turn around and see.

Kathy

Gossip

James 3:1-12

We humans are able to tame and **have tamed** all other **creatures** — wild animals and birds, reptiles and fish. But **no one** has ever been able to tame the **tongue.**

(James 3:7-8a)

A horse's bit. A ship's rudder. A small spark. A poisonous fang. A strange mix of images, isn't it? They are all something small, even seemingly insignificant in the big picture, but their size disguises their immense power.

A bit: a small piece of steel that turns a horse; a rudder: a flat piece of metal attached to the bottom of a boat's stern that forces the entire ship to move in a different direction; a spark: a flicker of fire that can begin a flame which consumes everything; the fang: a grooved tooth in a slithering wild animal that can kill.

James tells us that the tongue is like this: small and enormously useful, but wild and dangerous and powerful. With it we can sing and share ourselves with others and encourage friends and communicate needs. With it we

7

can gossip and spread hate and humiliate and offend others. How can this be? How can one small part of our bodies become an instrument both of worship and of war?

Is it kind? Is it true? Is it necessary? If you can't say yes to all three questions, bite it.

Our tongues bring up what is deep in our hearts. When we gossip, we're telling the truth, not about the other person, but about us. When we gossip, giving our tongues free rein, we only reveal the malice, hardheartedness, resentment, anger and insecurities we have inside. Our tongue both betrays us and hurts others.

And the strange thing is that the less we control our tongue, using it for evil instead of good, the more powerful and unruly and savage it becomes.

Next time your tongue is itching to wag, use the old taming rule: Is it kind? Is it true? Is it necessary? If you can't say yes to all three questions, bite it.

Lord, I hate it when I walk away from a conversation regretting something I said. But then there are moments when I've said something that really made you smile: a word of kindness, a humble apology, a costly truth, a song of praise. Lord, help me to shut my mouth to gossip and open it to goodness...

Lying

Genesis 20

Abimelech called Abraham and asked, "What have you done to us? What wrong have I done to you to make you bring this disaster on me and my kingdom? No one should ever do what you have done to me."

(Genesis 20:9)

It's just a fib, a white lie, a slight misrepresentation, a misleading impression, that's all. Let's not quibble about details. You misunderstood. It's a trivial thing, a minor deception for your own good.

Check out Abraham in today's story. You may call it a political maneuver, a creative strategy, an act of self-defense or temporary insanity. Abraham calls it a half-truth, since Sarah was his half-sister. Clever, but not good enough. God calls it like it is: a lie.

We do the same thing, waffling around the truth. At times the truth can be beautiful and nurturing; at other times it can be strategically disastrous, unlovely and painful. But the truth is never anything but the truth, and a lie is never anything but a lie. Like Abimelech's question in today's story, we ask: "Why do we do it?"

Look at Abraham's response. First, he had the impression that no one in the land feared God and that therefore they would have no qualms about killing him to get Sarah. Reason #1: We lie because we're afraid. Second, he reasoned that the pagan's lack of reverence for God would lead to sin, but he overlooked his own lack of reverence for God that also led to sin. Reason #2: We lie because we forget God.

> People who **tell the truth** are also people of courage and confidence and **self-control.**

Third, he figured that a partial truth was good enough. Reason #3: We lie because we do not understand the nature of truth, which is a priceless whole that has no value in pieces. Fourth, when Abraham remembered that "God sent him," and that God had a purpose for him, he concluded that the end justified the means. If Abimelech murdered him, it would thwart God's will, right? Reason #4: We lie because we want to control events according to our own understanding.

Four good reasons that deceive only us.

Lord, people who tell the truth are also people of courage and confidence and self-control. That's what I want to be. Shape me into a person of truth, a person with a reputation for absolute honesty. Make me bold but sensitive, just as you are with me...

Cheating

Genesis 27:1–28:10

Isaac answered, "Your brother came and **deceived me**. He has **taken away** your **blessing**."

(Genesis 27:35)

Cheating. It's become so common-place that it's practically expected. Surveys of students from high school through college show that the majority of them cheat frequently. When asked, students justify their behavior by pointing to the billionaire businessmen and women who have gained their fortunes by cheating. It's the way it's done, isn't it?

Sometimes we soften the word: bamboozle, gyp, swindle, fleece, dupe, bilk. These words imply that the victim (parent, sibling, teacher, employer, government) was a fool anyway, and it's his or her own fault.

We even admire clever cheaters: the one who can falsify a time card, who can get into the professor's computer system, who can get into the theater without paying, who can outfox the IRS, who can convince a parent that he or she made the curfew. It's creative planning, right?

You might think so upon first glance at today's story. Jacob is oh so smart; Esau is a dunderhead (it's his own fault) and Isaac is a sucker. Jacob simply took advantage of the opportunity that presented itself and, by the way, achieved God's purposes in the long run. Right? Hardly.

God's will could easily have been brought about without Jacob's cheating. The idea that God relies on our sin is ludicrous. The outcome of Jacob's choices? Jacob was exiled for 20 years. He probably never saw his mother again. He was repeatedly duped, in turn, by his father-in-law, who first cheated Jacob out of the woman he loved and then cheated him of his wages. And finally Jacob was cheated (by his own children) out of his beloved son, Joseph.

Cheat once, and you'll feel forced to cheat again.

There are two facts about cheating: 1) Cheating breeds cheating. Cheat once, and you'll feel forced to cheat again. Cheat on your homework assignments, and you'll need to cheat on your exams. 2) What you sow, you will reap. If you cheat, you will one day become the victim, the dupe, the fool. Just like Jacob.

It's so tempting to make things happen by a simple end-run around the rules. So many other people cheat that it doesn't seem to make much difference if I do it. In fact, I'm at a disadvantage if I don't! But you are there, God, right next to me hoping that I'll push through, do it on my own, claim true successes. Even an honest failure is better in your sight. Don't let me forget, God...

Stealing

Ephesians 4:28

If you **used to rob**, you must **stop robbing** and **start working...**

(Ephesians 4:28a)

There are as many reasons to steal as there are things to steal. Laziness, peer pressure, greed, jealousy, insecurity, fear, anger. There is always a reason whenever there's an opportunity.

The best reason seems to be that it just doesn't matter. After all, it's mostly minor things: an employer's supplies, a tube of lipstick, a box of Skittles, a pair of jeans. It's not like it really hurts anyone, is it? Business owners factor shoplifting into their prices, right?

But that pair of earrings slipped into the purse, that video carried under a coat, that box of computer paper loaded into your car—they do matter. Stealing is one of the Big Ten (commandments, that is), right after murder and adultery, and right before lying and coveting.

Stealing is part of that old self "that was being destroyed by its deceitful desires." It's destructive. It eats away

13

your innards and leads to moral rot. In today's verse, Paul describes the cure. It's not enough to shake the finger and say no, no. We're not children any more. It's not enough to grit the teeth and decide to be theft-free. A more potent cure is prescribed.

> The secret to **overcoming any temptation** is to replace it with a more **dynamic desire.**

A preacher once told the old Greek myth of Ulysses's temptation by the luring and fatal songs of half-human creatures. Ulysses tried to plug his ears so that he could resist their enchantment. Orpheus, on the other hand, did not worry about the songs' deadly charm. Instead of plugging his ears, he simply sang a song so much more beautiful, more powerful that the songs of the creatures were like screeching and squalling.

Paul understands this well. The secret to overcoming any temptation is to replace it with a more dynamic desire. Those who steal must stop stealing and turn their creative energies to earning enough to share with those in need. Followers of Christ who give up stealing and take up generosity, responsibility and hard work sing a powerful song.

Lord, how can you really care about something as trivial as a $10 cassette? But you do. I know you do. Small is not small to you, especially when it comes to secret places in my heart. Make me whole, Lord, so complete in you that I don't need to impress anyone else with my bravado and that I don't want what you don't freely give...

Family Pressure

Colossians 3:8-17

Clothe yourselves with compassion, **kindness,** humility, **gentleness**, and patience.

(Colossians 3:12b)

"**H**e drives me nuts!" "After all these years, she doesn't have a clue." "We just can't be in the same room for more than a few hours without an unkind word." "He doesn't give a rip about me."

You'd think these were the feelings of bitter enemies, but much of the time these are the words family members use to speak of one another. Counselors make a mint in the weeks after every major holiday because those are the times families gather again...and send each other up the wall again.

God did not create the home to be a gulag archipelago, a place of torment and frustration and isolation. The relationships you have with your siblings and your parents have the potential to be some of the safest, wisest, steadiest relationships you could have in life.

Paul describes this kind of community, a new level of relationship that can penetrate the family—your family. Paul knows that when we give in to selfish and unloving words or actions, we often destroy those who are closest to us. You know what he means: it has happened to you.

Call up all your energy... to change the destructive patterns in your home.

But this kind of community does not just beam down from above. It demands a commitment to aggressive holiness: an active, stubborn, canny approach to living and loving the ones in your home. And don't think it has to start with a parent. Maybe it should, but it might not. It can start with you.

"You are the people of God," Paul says. You, in the Spirit of Christ, can call up all your energy, your will and your talent to change the destructive patterns in your home.

When we work to live together in harmony, when we choose to act with kindness and patience, when we forgive others' brutish behavior and ask them to forgive our own, we discover that our relationships become peaceful, even holy.

God, it's hard to believe that I could change anything at home, and alone I know I can't. But with you...with what I know of your power and your desire for me and my relationships with my family...well, anything could happen. Make it happen in me first and then change us all. Make our family holy...

Conformity

Galatians 2:1-14

When Peter came to Antioch, **I opposed him** in public, because he was **clearly wrong**...The other Jewish believers also started **acting like cowards** along with Peter.

(Galatians 2:11, 13a)

Just when I think I've got it right, just when I'm truly convinced of the right thing to do, along comes that friend, that trusted mentor, that group of self-acclaimed experts who tell me that no, as a matter of fact, I'm wrong. Dead wrong. And that the right way to do things is, just by coincidence, their way of doing things. And then I get all confused. I felt so sure that I had figured it out, chosen the best way...

Peter knows just what you feel like when you try to do the right thing and have to struggle to stick to your guns. The early believers had to push through the expectations and assumptions of their Jewish background to reach a new understanding, a place of welcome and acceptance and even equality for—gasp!—Gentiles. Many of the new believers seemed to believe that, to be truly Christian, they had to keep all the Jewish laws, whether they were Jewish or not. Both Peter and Paul insisted that the only thing non-Jewish believers need to do to become children of God is to believe in Jesus and to show their faith by living lives of love.

Live like you believe...

and let them figure it out.

So Peter showed the truth by rubbing elbows at the dinner table with a bunch of Gentiles (something a good Jew would never do). But when some of his Jewish Christian friends came to visit, Peter started worrying about what they might think. The instant he focused on their opinions instead of his own convictions, he decided to stop hanging out with his Gentile friends.

Paul called him on it. Cowardly action. Hypocrisy. You know what is right, but you don't do it. You're willing to conform to the ignorance and stubbornness of others instead of choosing the high road of integrity. Paul says, "Walk a straight path in line with the truth of the gospel." Others won't like it—it's guaranteed. Live like you believe...and let them figure it out.

Lord, it's hard to swim upstream, and sometimes that's what I feel I have to do when my friends want me to do things their way. But you show me all the time that your way is the way of power and truth and beauty. One day I hope they will see things your way, the way I want to see them...

Waiting for God

1 Samuel 26

"God has put your enemy **in your power** tonight. Now let me plunge **his own spear** through him and pin him **to the ground...**"

(1 Samuel 26:8a)

Maybe you've had a glimpse of what you're called to do with your life. There's a hint of extraordinary talent, or a burning passion, or a hunger for discovery that drives you forward. It's there, just at the tip of your fingers, ready, waiting to be snatched...

Ever felt that anticipation? That itch? David knew it, and Saul read it all over his face. King Saul thinks that David is out to get his throne (which he is). So King Saul has been hunting David all over Israel (without much luck). Saul has been told that the kingdom will be taken from him and given to a man after God's own heart, a man who will do all that God wants him to do. David is that man, and both David and Saul know it.

Then a rare opportunity comes along, an opportunity to make it happen, a chance to be rid of Saul and become king in one swift move. The choice seems obvious, doesn't it? After all, David on the throne is God's plan.

David's friend, Abishai, encourages him to kill Saul. "Surely," Abishai suggests (with perfect sense, don't you think?), "this opportunity is straight from God. After all, you know God has chosen you to be king, and Saul has been trying to kill you. Do it!"

Make the **tough choice.** You can't **rush God.**

But David makes the harder choice. If God plans for Saul to drop dead, that's God's business, not David's. And God's business must happen in God's time.

David refuses to take advantage of his enemy; he refuses to doubt God's plan; he refuses to force God's hand. David chooses instead to wait: wait for Saul's choices to take their course and wait for God to fulfill the promise. Who knows what God might have done if David had ignored all that he knew about God, had reached past his love for God to grasp a special vision. Maybe God would have looked around for someone else to be king, someone who had the guts (and the heart) to stick with God. Make the tough choice. You can't rush God.

Lord, I do get so restless, wanting to push life along. And when I'm in that kind of a hurry, I get sloppy. It's hard to make wise choices when I'm rushing through life. Help me to slow down, watch for your hand, let you open doors...or close them. You know today and tomorrow, the good choice and the best choice, the dangers and possibilities. It's yours, God...

Suicide

Acts 16:22-34

The jailor...pulled out his sword and was about **to kill himself.**

(Acts 16:27)

In late 1995, two young lovers committed suicide. The parents believed they were getting too serious and were too young to make commitments, so they prohibited their children from seeing each other.

It has overtones of "Romeo and Juliet" and it sounds romantic, but it's not. Suicide is the most shortsighted choice a person can make. These two young people couldn't see. They couldn't see a future with possibilities, enormous, wonderful, beautiful possibilities. All they saw was frustration and sadness at being separated. The feelings are strong and real; the choice is weak and deceptive.

In the reading from Acts, Paul is the trigger for a man's attempted suicide. Paul's preaching lands him and his friend, Silas, in jail, where they are brutally beaten and chained. When an earthquake shakes the prison, opens all the cell doors, and unlocks the chains (clearly a divine act), the prison guard is sure that all the prisoners have escaped.

The guard thinks the game is up. Back then, if a prisoner escaped, the guard paid for it...permanently. So the guard decides to commit suicide rather than face the humiliation and terror of waiting for his own execution. Only Paul's sudden call keeps the guard from running his sword through himself.

Sometimes we can't see a guarantee for our happiness and so we lose hope.

"Don't harm yourself! We are all here!" Paul cries. Maybe we should all memorize these words. They are words of reassurance, of hope, of great comfort. Maybe there's someone you know who needs to hear them. Maybe it's you.

The guard didn't see the prisoners and so lost hope. Sometimes we can't see a guarantee for our happiness and so we lose hope. But the Lord is near, and so are many, many people who are "all here," wanting to help us, like the prison guard, discover new faith.

Lord, I want to be strong, both for myself and for those around me who need my words of reassurance. Help me to see, really see, the power and love and promise of your goodness for tomorrow and for all the days to come...

Family Violence

Ephesians 5:21, 6:1-4

Submit yourselves to one another because of your reverence **for Christ.**

(Ephesians 5:21)

It starts with little kids coming to second grade without any breakfast because no one bothered to feed them. Parents tell their children that they're worthless because their parents didn't care about them.

Then we hear our friend's mother and her live-in boyfriend scream obscenities and threaten violence. And our other friend's father abuses her. And on and on it goes. A bitter and painful cycle where everyone is a victim.

Ephesians paints an extraordinary picture. The writer seems to know that loving relationships within a family depend on mutual humility. As soon as one person, whether it's a parent or child, "gets the upper hand," the whole family gets out of whack.

In the family that honors Christ, parent submits to child by offering patient and gentle discipline and instruction. Child submits to parent through obedience and respect. Parent honors child; child honors parent.

A family is a shield. Each protects and cares for the other. Each makes promises and keeps them.

Such a family is a shield. Each protects and cares for the other. Each makes promises and keeps them. In the family, they find security and safety.

Perhaps your family is a far cry from the one in Ephesians. But the decisions you make today can lead to your own creation of such a family in the future.

God, sometimes it just seems like people thrive on hurting other people. Moms scream at little kids in the grocery store; friends come to school with bruises; the newspapers are full of pain. All I know is that this is not what you want, not for me and not for anyone else either. Teach me now how to honor the ones I love so that I'll be ready one day to build a home on mutual respect...

Gangs

Genesis 37:12-34

"Come on now, **let's kill him** and **throw his body** into one of the dry wells."

(Genesis 37:20a)

Gangs are nothing new. They're just one more way for people to feel okay doing something together that the individuals in the group are smart enough not to do alone.

Joseph knows all about gangs. His half-brothers were such a gang. And they spit on Joseph in their dreams. Maybe they had once put the pressure on Joseph to stop being such a goody-two-shoes and join them. Who knows?

In Genesis 37, this gang takes Joseph out. They "plot against him and decide to kill him." But instead of killing Joseph, they decide to profit from his disappearance and sell him to some slave traders heading for Egypt. "Whew!" they must have thought. "That takes care of that little pest."

Little do they understand about how God works. As Joseph—who ends up as the ruler of all Egypt—later says, "You plotted evil against me, but God turned it into good."

Gangs don't impress God. God has seen plenty of gang members come and go.

Gangs don't impress God. God has seen plenty of gang members come and go. God had a plan for Joseph, the victim; and God had a plan for his brothers, the gang members. And nothing got in God's way, certainly not a bunch of people trying to protect their bit of turf.

Lord, it's hard to see your plans at work when I hear about gangs today. But then, I don't imagine Joseph had any idea what you were doing either. Give me Joseph's faith, Joseph's confidence...the certainty that you are working in all the events of my life...

Selfishness to Savagery

Judges 19

"**No**, my friends! Please! Don't do such an **evil, immoral thing!**"

(Judges 19:23)

We thrive on violent movies, violent stories in the news, violent showdowns on the streets and violent cartoons. Deep down we know that this is nothing new. Violence is in the human heart and we need a transplant.

Judges 19 doesn't hide the truth. Totally gruesome: rape, beating, death, dismemberment. The story continues through the end of the book: revenge, war, massacre, kidnapping. It rivals any story you'll read in today's newspapers. And even those who seem most appalled continue to demonstrate complete disregard for women, even in their attempts to patch it all up.

How on earth did this get into the Bible? It just goes to show that God is not blind, deaf and dumb. God is very aware of the depths of our depravity. Nothing shocks God. The whole book of Judges shows God's people wallowing in evil and needing God to rescue them. One little sentence, echoed here and there in the book, tells all: "In those days there was no king in Israel; all the people did what was right in their own eyes."

> **I do have a King, and I'm called to do what is right in his eyes, not my own.**

It's said a hundred different ways: "Whatever you think is right." "I gotta live my own life." "Hey, as long as you're sincere." "Do your own thing."

Judges shows us where such thinking can lead.

Lord, the world tries to tell me that it's okay to do whatever I want to do to make myself feel good. But I do have a King, and I'm called to do what is right in his eyes, not my own. Sometimes it seems like the world has gone nuts and can't tell right from wrong. But you are King, Lord, and I want to live under your leadership...

Guns

1 Samuel 17:41-51

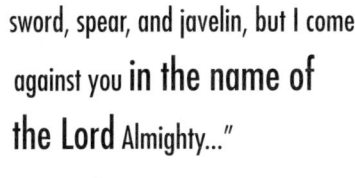

David answered, "You are **coming against me** with sword, spear, and javelin, but I come against you **in the name of the Lord** Almighty..."

(1 Samuel 17:45a)

We drive down the street and see a car with four or five young guys in it, hard rock music blaring away, and wonder: "How many guns are in that car? What if I get in the way?" Then we begin to think that maybe we ought to get a gun, too, just to protect ourselves.

Talk about keeping up with the Joneses. It's crazy. And it's deadly. Guns make people feel like Goliath—confident, arrogant, aggressive, hostile. Like him, such people swagger forward, daring anyone to cross their paths.

Here comes David. We might feel like him. Small. Unarmed. Goliath "was filled with scorn for him because he was just a nice, good-looking boy." Sort of like the Terminator against Wally Cleaver.

In the face of crude threats, overwhelming force and a barrage of obscenities, David stands serene and fearless. He draws on his experience in defending his sheep from lions and bears, and he knows God has prepared him for this battle too. David has a secret weapon: the power of God that is ours when we walk in God's ways.

Comparing a gun's deadly force to your intense power is like comparing a bee sting to an exploding star.

"The Lord does not need swords or spears [or handguns, we might add] to save his people."

God, guns are so tangible and you're so, well, so hidden. Guns are hard and cold and heavy; you are secret and subtle and silent. But deep down I know that comparing a gun's deadly force to your intense power is like comparing a bee sting to an exploding star. I'm on your side, Lord, because I know you're on mine. Give me the bravery of boy David...

Spiritualism

1 Samuel 28:4-20

"Consult the spirits for me and tell me what is going to happen," he said to her. "Call up the spirit of the man I name."

(1 Samuel 27:8b)

King Saul had been "over the edge" for some time. Not long after he was crowned as king of Israel, he began to slip. A little impatience here, a shortcut to glory there, and a lingering tendency to justify his disobedience by trying to improve on God's instructions. 1 Samuel paints a sad picture of Saul as a man who just didn't make the extra effort to obey God.

So now Saul is a terrified man: he's afraid of God, of David, of his friends and of his enemies. He needs power; he needs guidance; he needs to regain control. But his own reluctance to side completely with God has left him vulnerable to confusion.

What to do in a moment of panic? Of course, do yet another thing that God has forbidden: consult a medium, a witch, who promised to conjure up for Saul the spirit of the dead prophet, Samuel.

Does it help? Does it offer Saul any advantage over his enemies? No; his last foolish decision robs him of all hope. Not long after, Saul totters over the brink of despair and commits suicide.

I know that even that innocent exploration can get me into a real mess.

God's command that we reject spiritualism, communication with the dead and other psychic powers is not just a divine head trip. It is God's way of protecting and guiding us.

God knows the human thirst for power and control in our lives. But when we close our hearts to the promises of power that comes with spiritualism, we open ourselves to be vessels of God's power, which brings health and life and happiness.

Lord, sometimes it's mere curiosity that makes me want to explore things like channeling or seances or tarot cards. But I know that even that innocent exploration can get me into a real mess. Help me to save my curiosity for you, because you are a wonder and a surprise and an unending source of discovery and delight...

Divination

Daniel 2:1-30

"Your Majesty, there is no wizard, magician, fortuneteller, or astrologer who can tell you that. But there is a God in heaven, who reveals mysteries."

(Daniel 2:27-28a)

Do you think it would be great to know the future? Imagine it for a minute. You could make a fortune on the stock market. You could always make decisions that lead to bliss. You could prevent horrible things from happening. You could prepare for natural disasters. It would be fantastic!

Or would it? Why do you think God makes creation march onward through time, one day following another, none of us really knowing what the next day will bring?

Maybe it's God's sense of adventure, God's love of risk. I mean, not having everything mapped out for us does keep us living on the edge.

Maybe it's a way of keeping us in a faithful, trusting relationship with God. Daniel believed this and proved to Nebuchadnezzar, king of the Babylonians, that God alone knows the future.

Nebuchadnezzar was used to hearing the advice of his fortunetellers, magicians, sorcerers and wizards. But when a troubling dream haunted him, they were worthless.

God's **love of mystery** can surprise us and delight us, if we're willing to **trust God** with tomorrow.

Daniel knows that the mysteries of life, including the future, belong to God. It doesn't mean God is just being nasty, making us sweat it out. On the contrary, God's love of mystery can surprise us and delight us, if we're willing to trust God with tomorrow.

Lord, it seems like it would be great to avoid all the pain and frustration and sadness that comes in life. But clearly my fumbling faith in the midst of it all pleases you. I'm amazed at both your patience and your expectations. Lead me day by day into the mysteries of life that you've prepared for me...

Fantasy Games

2 Samuel 12:1-13

The Lord sent **the prophet Nathan** to David. Nathan went to him and said, **"There were two men** who lived in the same town; one was **rich** and the other **poor..."**

(2 Samuel 12:1)

Little children roleplay all the time. They make-believe real situations, like house and doctor and cops and robbers; and they make-believe fantasy stories, like mermaids and princesses and dinosaur hunts. This is the way children learn about real life.

As we leave childhood, this natural ability to play is stifled within us. We're told to "grow up," to act like an adult, to quit pretending. How sad to unlearn the gift of play and telling stories and imagining.

The Bible knows the power of stories. It is a Story, and it's full of stories. And those stories can change us, as this reading shows. Nathan, God's prophet, relies on a simple story to open David's stubborn heart to God. David had done some dreadful things: slept with another man's wife and then sent the husband back to the war carrying his own death warrant.

My mind is a **marvelous thing**, and so I want to direct **all my energies** toward the power of good, **your good.**

Nathan knows that direct confrontation would probably have been a waste of time. Instead, he tells a tale of a ruthless man who took another man's pet and ate it for dinner. Unknowingly, David condemns himself, and is then open to repentance and forgiveness.

The power of imagination can be used for good or evil. Make-believe goodness in your life, and you may find that holy play leads to holiness.

God, a lot of people really get into these games, and it's hard to see anything wrong with most of them. But I know my mind is a marvelous thing, and so I want to direct all my energies toward the power of good, your good. Help me to figure out what games are worth my mind, and which ones aren't...

The Power of Music

Isaiah 55:1-9

"Why **spend money** on what **does not satisfy?"**

(Isaiah 55:2a)

A famous director and composer once wrote, "Extraordinary how potent cheap music is." Potent is just the right word. Music, good and bad, can act like a drug: it can change our moods, lift our spirits, create feelings of sadness or hilarity or romance or anger. We all have certain songs that seem to invade us in a special way. "They're playing our song!"

Music seems to quench a certain thirst we have, a desire to express and explore our feelings. God certainly understands this human characteristic. Maybe that's why the longest book in the Bible, the Psalms, is really a songbook.

This longing reveals our inner need for life and love and affirmation and celebration. Problems begin to crop up when we look in all the wrong places for what we need.

37

That's what happened to God's people. They spent all
their time and energy and money and hope on things

Our choices in music can lead us closer to God or leave us empty.

that didn't satisfy them. Isaiah
records God's offer: Come!
Change your way of thinking.
Quench your thirst here, with Me.

We often make the same weak
decisions. We waste our money and our time on things
that do not enhance our relationship with God.

Music has the power to change us, and our choices in
music can lead us closer to God or leave us empty.

"Why spend your wages and still be hungry?"

Jesus, sometimes a song can draw out of me some feelings that lie so deep they can't be expressed any other
way. Sometimes it feels great and sometimes it frightens
me. Do something down inside of me where these feelings are coming from. Help me to choose music that lets
me feel you, your love and joy and peace...

Divorce

Psalm 27

My father and mother may **abandon me,** but the
Lord will **take care** of me.

(Psalm 27:10)

A mother calmly explained the word
divorce to her 5-year-old daughter. "It means
that Uncle Jack and Aunt Linda are getting
unmarried." The little girl thought about it
for a minute, and then blurted out, "But
what about Debbie and Ryan? Don't
Uncle Jack and Aunt Linda love their children any more?"

Though only 5 years old, the little girl had a keen understanding of what marriage is all about: a circle of love
and commitment that can't be broken without hurting
everyone.

Chances are you've been hurt by divorce in some way.
Maybe it's a part of your own family's experience; maybe it has invaded the lives of other family members or of
your friends; maybe it has ravaged your admiration of a
mentor or teacher or leader who had an excellent marriage...or so you thought.

It's not the way it was meant to be. A circle, like the wedding ring, has no beginning and no end. So, once marriage becomes divorce, once the circle is snapped, what happens to the broken pieces?

Nothing changes God's powerful love, which is always present.

The psalmist believes that all our feelings of abandonment, of loneliness, of need or of fear are like empty jars that God is longing to fill. The emptier we become, the greater the opportunity.

Listen: "The Lord protects me from all danger; I will never be afraid."

"In times of trouble God will shelter me."

"Trust in the Lord. Have faith, do not despair."

A lot of things happen in this life that do not make God happy. Divorce is one of them. But nothing, absolutely nothing, changes God's powerful love, which is always present in our lives and in our parents' lives. That love will triumph.

Lord, I hate the pain that is all around me because of divorce. It makes me angry and restless and afraid. I want to lash out and hurt the ones who have hurt me. Remind me, Lord, of your willingness to heal me and those I love from this hurt. Help me to know that all is not lost. You can bring good out of all our mistakes...

Changing Relationships

Ecclesiastes 3:1-14

He sets the time for **finding** and the time for **losing,** the time for **saving** and the time for **throwing away...**

(Ecclesiastes 3:6)

Ｈow odd it is the way we drift in and out of each others' lives, clinging and loving and needing and then letting go, out of sight and out of mind. How does that happen?

We humans are curious about this fluidity, this movement of time on our deepest feelings. We laugh about it when we watch sitcoms that poke fun at the on-again-off-again nature of our friendships; we cry about it when they **are** dramatized for us as mini-series; we are enthralled by it when they are exaggerated on soap operas.

Still, it's odd. Your best friend in elementary school no longer acknowledges you in the hall. You and your junior high buddy don't have anything in common any more. When you graduate from high school, the ones you miss the most will surely fade from your affections, if not your memory. Then, someday, you won't recognize your dearest college friends at a reunion. We're blessed if we keep even one friend for a lifetime.

As humans we must accept the changes that space and time bring us.

The reading from Ecclesiastes consoles us in our losses. The author explains to us that as humans we must accept the changes that space and time bring us. But it feels uncomfortable because God has set eternity in our hearts. We see it; we reach for it; but it is not ours, at least for now. Only God is eternal, constant, unchanging.

Ecclesiastes' advice is good: Enjoy the friends you have. They may not remain forever. Do not think of it as losing love, but as gathering and storing love. For "everything God does will last forever." When your friendships change and seem to pass away, know that what was good and right and perfect in them, what was created by God, will remain. A time will come...

Lord, time is weird, and the reality of growing out of a friendship is strange. I feel a real sense of loss, and I wonder if I could have done something different to make it last. But I am not in control of all my relationships; they seem to have a life of their own. Help me to mourn their passing with grace, clinging firmly to the One whose love for me never ends...

Dedication to God

Genesis 22:1-19

"Take your son," God said, "**your only son**, Isaac, whom you **love so much**, and...**offer him** as a sacrifice to me."

(Genesis 22:2)

Humans have an incredible capacity for intensity in every aspect of life. We rarely use it.

A lot of people exercise. Some are into sports. A few could be considered athletes. And then there are the Olympians, men and women who have dedicated themselves to the perfect discipline of their bodies.

A lot of people study. Some are really into learning. A few could be considered intellectual. And then there are the scholars, men and women who have dedicated themselves to the perfect discipline of their minds.

Most of us are not very intense about anything much.

A lot of people believe in God. Some are pretty religious. A few could be considered active and sincere

Christians. And then there are the saints, men and women who have dedicated all of themselves to the perfect love of God.

God, sometimes your love for me is frightening.

People admire athletes and Olympians; people esteem intellectuals and scholars; people sneer at saints. They use words like fanatics, loonies, extremists. If they're conservative, they're called fundamentalists. If they're liberal, they're called radicals. Either way, we reduce them to a label.

Abraham is a saint. He begins by listening to God's voice. He then takes a step into the unknown by leaving his home for a place God would show him. He then pushes his faith further, trusting God for a son even though he and Sarah were way past childbearing age.

In this reading we see how far Abraham's dedication to God will go. It pushes all the limits. He gives up the son he loves; he lets go of God's promises about an heir; he risks it all; he withholds nothing. Why? Because Abraham is dedicated completely to God.

You're past the place of mere believing. God invites you to be a saint.

God, sometimes your love for me is frightening. It is so demanding, so vast, so hungry! Help me to see that your love is perfect and gentle and patient, accepting me now, today, just as I am and inviting me deeper into your love, straight into your heart...

Death

Revelation 21:1-7

"There will be no more death, no more grief or crying or pain."

(Revelation 21:4b)

Space is not the final frontier; death is. Someday we will all become explorers.

We can guess about death; we can entertain rumors of those who have glimpsed it and returned; we can talk about stages of grief and about time healing all wounds. But when you bury someone you love, you need more than that.

God does not give us details about death and resurrection and what happens to the spirit in between. God does give us certain promises: that in Christ all will be made alive; that the dead in Christ will rise and that we will be reunited with them.

This reading from Revelation reminds us that death is not permanent. God has a goal: to live among us; to rid creation of all the old things, like death and crying and pain; to "wipe away all tears from our eyes."

What does this image do to your soul when it weeps uncontrollably: God stoops down, takes a handkerchief from a pocket, gently lifts your chin and wipes your tears? What does this say about God? about what God wants for you? about what God wants for those whom you love?

Rest in God, who not only holds those we have **loved** and lost, but **keeps them** for a future day.

When you face death, when its cold fingers pry open your pleasant life and squeeze out all the joy and love and hope so that everything is broken and empty and over, then rest in God, who not only holds those we have loved and lost, but keeps them for a future day.

To that brightest of all meetings, bring us!

Lord, it's one thing to lose a friendship; it's another to lose a friend. I can't bear the pain of the empty place that death has brought. The only one I want to talk to about my feelings is the one who is gone. No one else understands. Except you. Here, Lord, take my tears and loneliness and endless longing. Hasten the day when they're replaced with the delight of reunion...

Scripture Index